DON'T STAND WHERE THE COMET IS ASSUMED TO STRIKE OIL

Other DILBERT Books from BOXTREE

TREASURIES

Fugitive From the Cubicle Police
ISBN: 0-7522-2431-X

Seven Years of Highly Defective People
ISBN: 0-7522-2407-7

What Do You Call a Sociopath In a Cubicle? Answer: A Coworker
ISBN: 0-7522-2417-4

Dilbert Gives You the Business
ISBN: 0-7522-2394-1

Dilbert – A Treasury of Sunday Strips: Version 00
ISBN: 0-7522-7232-2

It's Obvious You Won't Survive by Your Wits Alone
ISBN: 0-7522-0201-4

COLLECTIONS

Excuse Me While I Wag
ISBN: 0-7522-2399-2

When Did Ignorance Become a Point of View?
ISBN: 0-7522-2412-3

Journey to Cubeville
ISBN: 0-7522-2384-4

Build a Better Life by Stealing Office Supplies
ISBN: 0-7522-0716-4

Shave the Wales
ISBN: 0-7522-0849-7

Bring Me the Head of Willy the Mailboy!
ISBN: 0-7522-0136-0

Dogbert's Clues for the Clueless
ISBN: 0-7522-0711-3

Words You Don't Want to Hear During Your Annual Performance Review
ISBN: 0-7522-2422-0

Another Day In Cubicle Paradise
ISBN: 0-7522-2486-7

Random Acts of Management
ISBN: 0-7522-7174-1

Don't Step in the Leadership
ISBN: 0-7522-2389-5

I'm Not Anti-Business, I'm Anti-Idiot
ISBN: 0-7522-2379-8

Casual Day Has Gone Too Far
ISBN: 0-7522-1119-6

Still Pumped from Using the Mouse
ISBN: 0-7522-2265-1

Always Postpone Meetings with Time-Wasting Morons
ISBN: 0-7522-0854-3

When Body Language Goes Bad
ISBN: 0-7522-2491-3

BEST OF DILBERT

The Best of Dilbert Volume 1
ISBN: 0-7522-6541-5

Best of Dilbert Volume 2
ISBN: 0-7522-1500-0

For ordering information, call 01624 677237

DILBERT

DON'T STAND WHERE THE COMET IS ASSUMED TO STRIKE OIL

A DILBERT BOOK
BY SCOTT ADAMS

BOXTREE

First published 2004 by Andrews McMeel Publishing, an Andrews McMeel Universal company, Kansas City, USA

First published in Great Britain 2004 by Boxtree
an imprint of Pan Macmillan Ltd
Pan Macmillan, 20 New Wharf Road, London N1 9RR
Basingstoke and Oxford
Associated companies throughout the world
www.panmacmillan.com

ISBN 0 7522 2402 6

1 3 5 7 9 8 6 4 2

A CIP catalogue record for this book is available from
the British Library.

Printed and bound in Great Britain by
The Bath Press Ltd, Bath

For a woman who thinks *crafts* and *crap* are completely different concepts

Introduction

You've probably noticed that the population of earth can be divided into smart people and dumb people. That would be a handy distinction if there were any way you could tell which group you were in. I mean, how can you know whether you are really a smart person or actually so dumb that you think you are smart? I have to assume it all feels the same.

It's easier to tell if other people are dumb. A good test is to announce at your next gathering that you have discovered an herbal treatment for ugliness, fatness, baldness, impotence, hair loss, and unhappiness. Say that it involves eating grass while repeating a special mantra in your head: "moo."

Dumb people will assume that you are highly qualified to dispense medical advice, especially if you say you tried something and it worked, or you saw it on *Oprah*. Then they'll drop on all fours and scurry out to the backyard to begin the cure. Smart people will ask you what scientific evidence you have to back up your ridiculous claim. That's where the fun begins. I like to take that conversation in this direction:

Smart Person: What evidence do you have of your claim?

Me: What evidence do you have of anything you think you know?

Smart Person: I rely on scientific evidence.

Me: How many double-blind studies have you performed?

Smart Person: Well, none, but I read about them.

Me: So you rely on writers you don't know to describe research you don't fully understand, performed by people who often have financial incentives to mislead you?

Smart Person: You have exposed me for the hypocrite and fraud that I am. I'll be out on the lawn.

Me: Very good. Stay away from the grass near the trees. We have dogs.

Actually, it doesn't usually have that happy ending. There's typically some blather about repeatable results, peer reviews, and how science isn't perfect but it's better than guessing, blah, blah, blah. Then I point out how it all boils down to "someone that you don't know told you it was true." Pretty soon there are fisticuffs, corrective lenses go flying, children cry. My point is that I don't get invited to parties and I don't know why.

But you're invited to the only party that counts. If you sign up for the free *Dilbert* newsletter, written by me whenever I feel like it—usually five times a year—then you will automatically be a member of Dogbert's New Ruling Class. When Dogbert conquers the world, you will be in the ruling elite just like you always wanted to be.

To subscribe, go to www.Dilbert.com and follow the links. If you have any trouble subscribing, send an e-mail to newsletter@unitedmedia.com.

S.Adams

Scott Adams

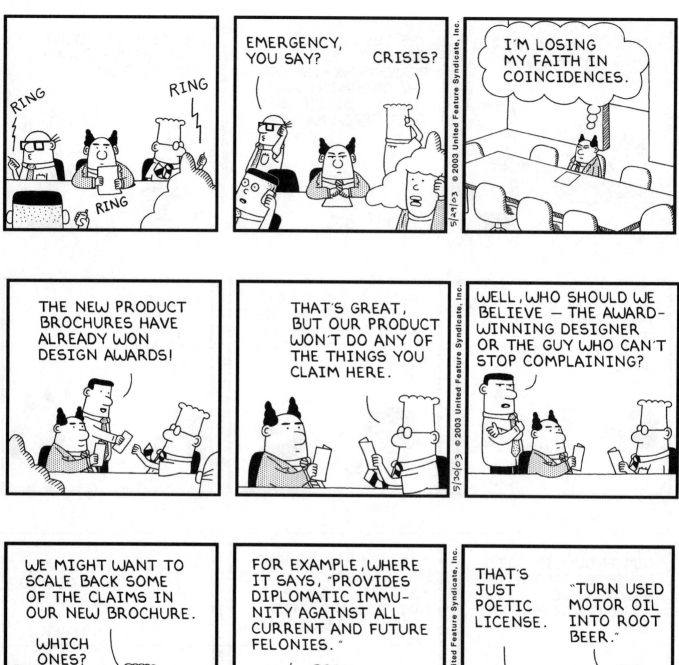

THE COMPANY WILL BE TAKING A ONE-TIME CHARGE TO WRITE DOWN THE VALUE OF OUR MERGER.

THE NUMBER IS SO LARGE THAT IT HAS NO NAME. OUR MARKETING DEPARTMENT IS ON IT.

LET'S SEE A SHOW OF HANDS FOR "FROOGLEPOOPILLION."

WE NEED TO ANNOUNCE OUR RECORD LOSSES IN A WAY THAT DOESN'T MAKE MANAGEMENT LOOK LIKE...

INEBRIATED SIMIAN MISCREANTS?

RIGHT.

GRAPHICS DEPARTMENT

THEY WANT TO GO IN A WHOLE OTHER DIRECTION.

A GOOD MANAGER NEEDS TO SMELL LIKE A MANAGER.

YOUR BREATH SHOULD BE A FIERY CONCOCTION THAT SAYS, "AGREE WITH ME OR DIE."

TRY "DOGBERT'S MANAGEMENT BREATH ENHANCER," MADE FROM GROUND-UP CIGARETTES, FARM SHOVELS AND COFFEE.

29

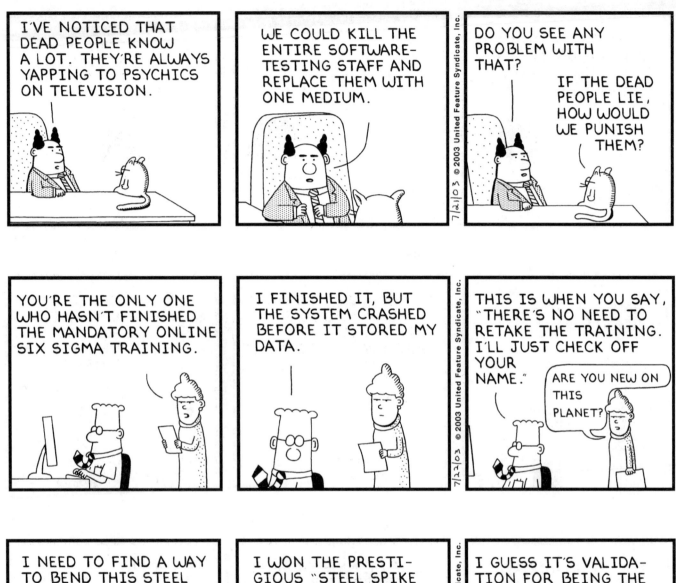

OUR NEW AD CAMPAIGN WILL USE FAMILIAR MUSIC FROM ARTISTS WHO ARE WILLING TO SELL OUT.

DUE TO BUDGET CUTS, WE'LL LIMIT OUR SEARCH TO MUSICIANS WHO ARE DEAD BUT NOT YET TOTALLY DECOMPOSED.

MAKEUP!!!

AS YOU REQUESTED, THIS PRICE QUOTE INCLUDES ABSOLUTELY EVERY EXPENSE YOU'LL INCUR!

IF THAT'S TRUE, YOU WON'T MIND SIGNING THE "ALICE SIDE AGREEMENT."

"IN THE EVENT OF HIDDEN COSTS, CUSTOMER WILL REPEATEDLY PUNCH VENDOR WHILE YELLING 'YOU FREAKING WEASEL!'"

PEN?

YOU LAUGH AT EVERYTHING, WHETHER IT'S FUNNY OR NOT.

HA HA HA!! IT'S TRUE.

YOU'RE HIRED. YOU'LL HAVE A BIG IMPACT ON MORALE!

HA HA HA!! YES, I WILL!

MUST STAY ALIVE.

HA HA HA!! COMPUTERS ARE FUNNY! HA HA!!

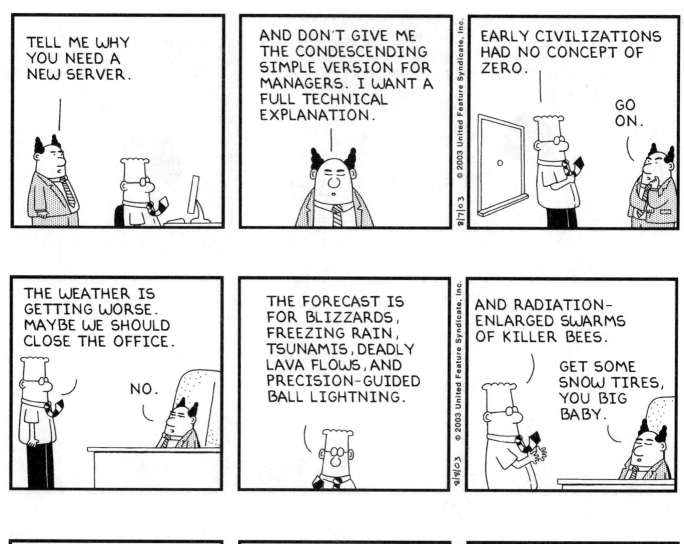

47

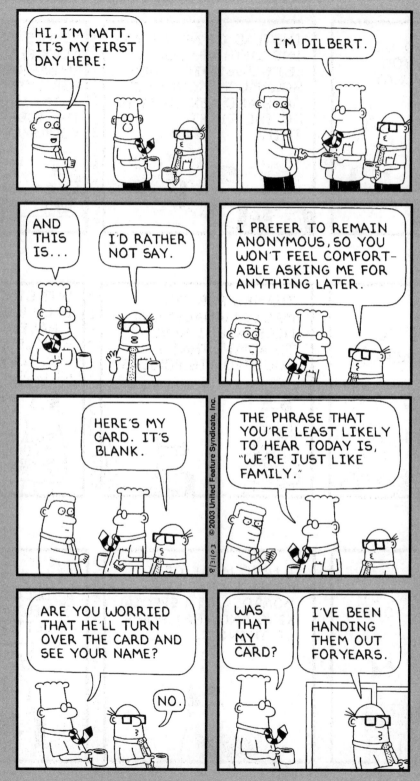

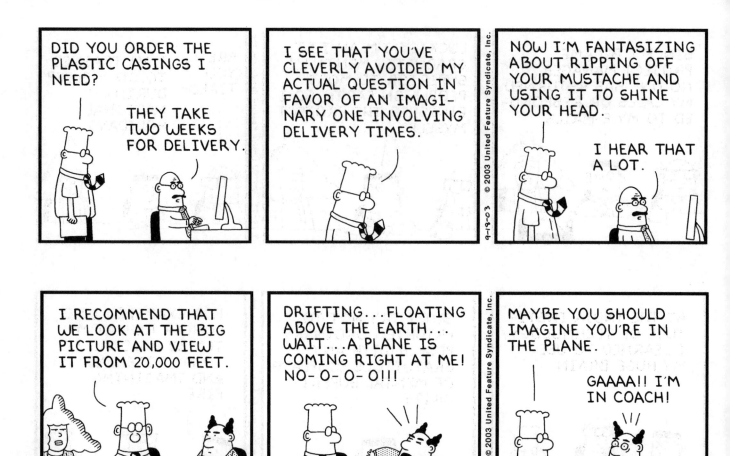

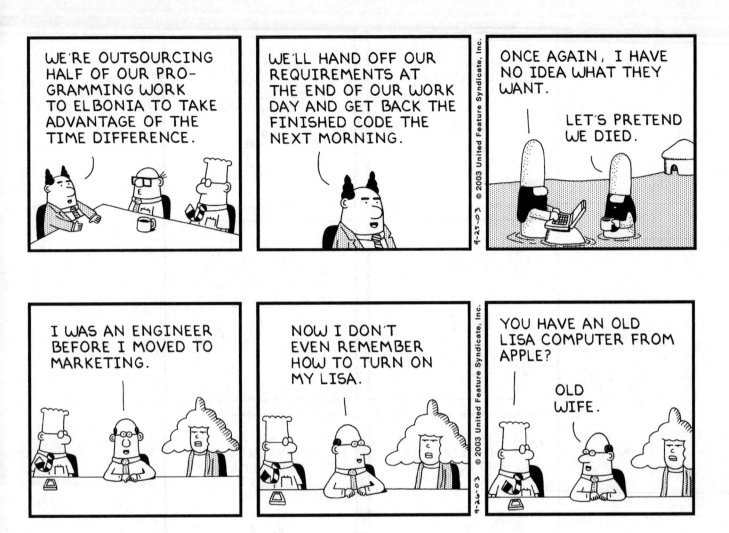

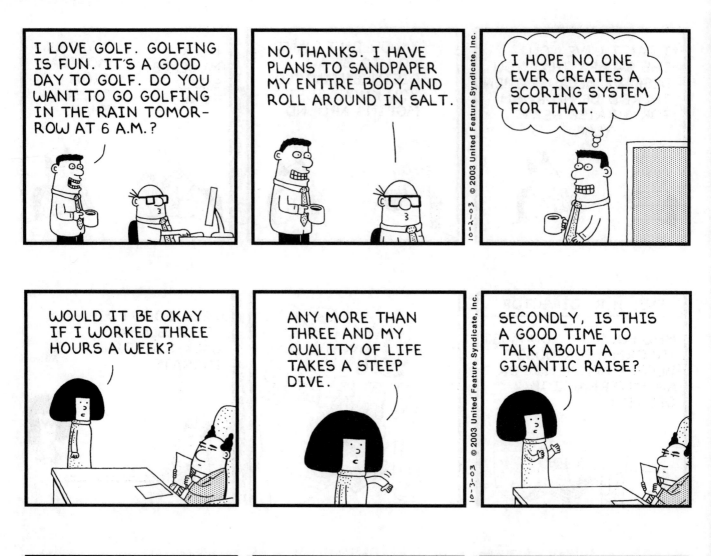

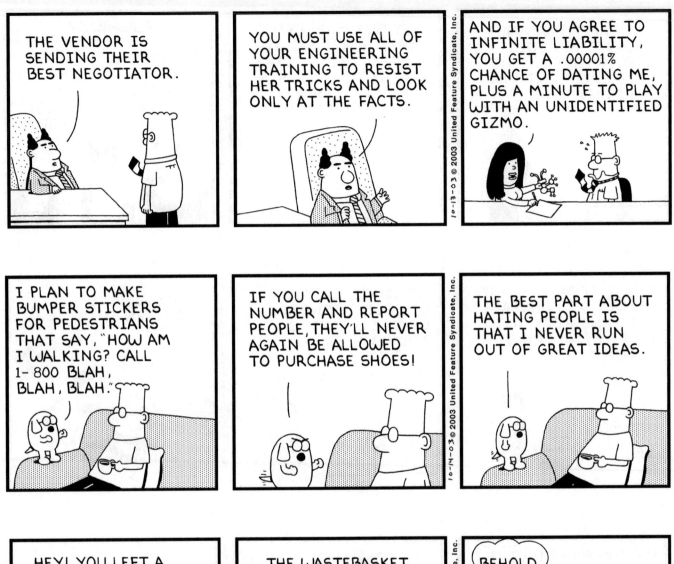

Panel 1: I CAN'T IMAGINE WHAT YOU TOLD EVERYONE AT THE MANAGEMENT RETREAT...

Panel 2: BUT OUR MARKETING DEPARTMENT ISSUED A PRESS RELEASE SAYING WE'RE DESIGNING A TUNNEL LINKING EUROPE TO DENVER.

Panel 3: FLASHBACK

I'M INSTALLING A NEW SPRINKLER SYSTEM IN MY LAWN.

MUST TOP.

Panel 4: I CALL IT THE "TUNNEL SHARK." IT CONVERTS DIRT AND ROCK INTO ENERGY AND CAN DIG FOREVER.

Panel 5: SO WHATEVER YOU DO, DON'T IGNORE WHAT I'M SAYING AND PUSH THE RED BUTTON.

BUTTON!

Panel 6: NOW WHAT'S GOTTEN INTO YOU?

Panel 7: 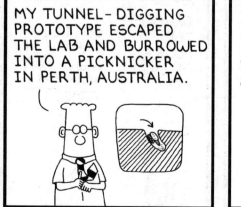 MY TUNNEL-DIGGING PROTOTYPE ESCAPED THE LAB AND BURROWED INTO A PICKNICKER IN PERTH, AUSTRALIA.

Panel 8:  THE COMBINED ENTITY IS A CYBORG THAT HAS PROVEN TO BE SURPRISINGLY POPULAR AT PARTIES.

Panel 9:  HA HA! DO THE TRICK WITH THE DIRT!

71

LYNN JOHNSTON, *For Better or For Worse*

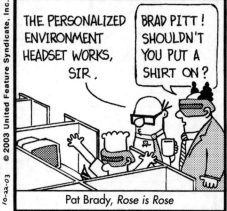

Darby Conley, *Get Fuzzy*

Pat Brady, *Rose is Rose*

72

86

95

THE GOOD THING ABOUT BEING DOWNSIZED IS THAT I DON'T NEED TO SHAVE MY LEGS.

IT GROWS FAST, BUT WHO'S GOING TO NOTICE?

POLICE SURROUNDED A CONVENIENCE STORE WHERE SASQUATCH ATTEMPTED TO BUY "HÄAGEN DAZS®."

BUSINESS IS PICKING UP. WE NEED TO REHIRE SOME OF THE PEOPLE THAT WE DOWNSIZED.

I HOPE THE TIME OFF FROM WORK HASN'T DULLED THEIR ENGINEERING INSTINCTS.

THE FIRST DAY BACK IS ALWAYS THE HARDEST.

I SIGNED YOU UP FOR A PRODUCT AWARENESS CLASS.

GAAA!!!

THEY'LL GIVE YOU HANDS-ON TRAINING FOR EVERY PRODUCT WE SELL.

PLE-E-EASE...

WE'RE HOPING TO FIX THIS PROBLEM IN THE NEXT VERSION.

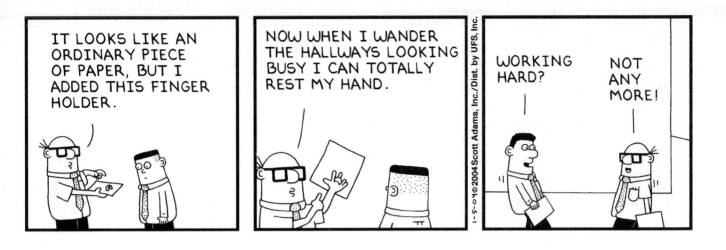

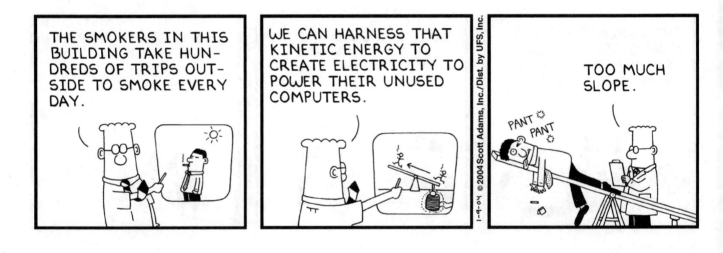

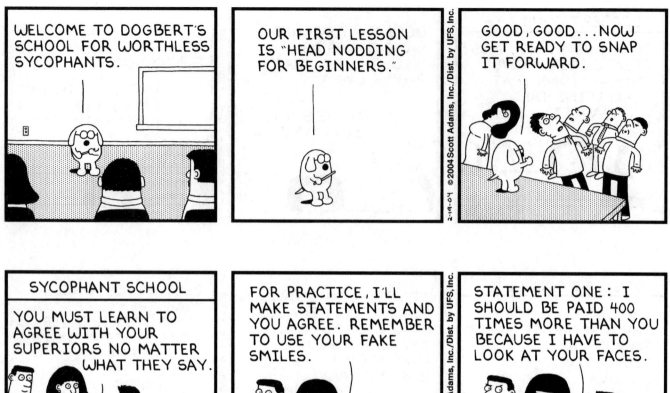